self-portrait without a bicycle

SELF-PORTRAIT WITHOUT A BICYCLE

JESSICA HIEMSTRA

POEMS

BIBLIOASIS

FIRST EDITION

Library and Archives Canada Cataloguing in Publication

Hiemstra, Jessica, 1979-

    Self-portrait without a bicycle / Jessica Hiemstra.

Poems.

ISBN 978-1-926845-90-6

    I. Title.

PS8615.I363S44 2012   C811'.6   C2012-901711-6

Readied for the press by Eric Ormsby
Copy-edited by Tara Murphy
Cover art and drawings by Jessica Hiemstra
Layout and design by Kate Hargreaves

 Canada Council Conseil des Arts
for the Arts du Canada

 Canadian Patrimoine
Heritage canadien

 ONTARIO ARTS COUNCIL
CONSEIL DES ARTS DE L'ONTARIO

Biblioasis acknowledges the ongoing financial support of the Government of Canada through the Canada Council for the Arts, Canadian Heritage, the Canada Book Fund; and the Government of Ontario through the Ontario Arts Council.

PRINTED AND BOUND IN CANADA

For Keira Jo
(I would have bought you a bicycle with red streamers)

contents

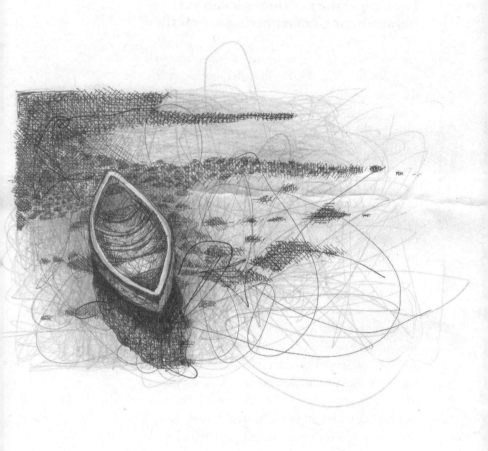

october
(the destruction of construction paper)

Looking at the sky through dahlias
(remembering remembering my mother)

I'm not sure how to pronounce *dahlia*—how stiff
to make the *a,* but I say it how my mom says it,
the way I leave butter on the rim of a white plate,
take a bath to soothe anger, soak it out. I sing
the way she sang *Graceland* all my growing-up,
Saturday mornings, breaking eggs. This morning
I caught myself failing at an omelet the way she does,
humming *but I have a reason to believe,* remembering
the two of us on the ferry leaving Freetown
this summer, a music video of Paul Simon on a little TV,
boogying in Soweto, diesel fumes and children's noses
pressed against glass. I sipped Fanta, the way I did

when I was small, looked at mom with more than love
because I was remembering my head in her lap, lamp-heat
on my cheek, the way she cleaned my ears humming
we both will be received as she curved the groove.
My vase of flowers on the table, dahlias
before mountains, makes me wish she was here.
She taught me to find the corridors—the curve
of mountain behind petal, how to curl my tongue
into the mixer for whip cream. She taught me
to save: not time or money, but pleasure—
how to find the world in a red dahlia, *in Graceland.*
Loveliness, one sip at a time, doesn't run out
or overflow.

Well, the cat's dead

i.

I wasn't fond of her but one dandelion in a jar
is pretty. One cat, grey and shy and mine
is more than a cat—it's a kind of love,
the way a dandelion yellow in glass is a kind of loyalty,
an admission of beauty. I remember her teats, kittens
pressing and milking. She hated the dog, silently
glared from the rafters. She's the last of the animals
I grew up with—outlived them all from the beams
of the barn hissing and preening, regal even
with her tongue in the naked part of her belly,
hind leg in the air. Dying isn't glorious

but she died in combat, fought a raccoon. Dad found her,
disembowelled. She expired purring in his lap
with a bowl of milk, intestines askew, swaddled tightly
in a blanket. My brother named her *Grayling*
after an English fish also called *the lady
of the stream.* The fish is nothing special,
just sleek and pretty, but I guess if I had one
in a jar on the table,
I'd owe it too, more.

ii.

So I got to thinking—Wikipedia says the grayling
has *the most beautiful dorsal fin of any fish*, but that could be
just a nostalgic fisher in England, slipping it in,
after too many drinks—loving an ordinary fish for love
of country and lager and because writing it down
makes it true. I don't know

much about England or fish. I had a cat once—that's all,
I thought she was nothing special
but it turns out that's never the case
with anything.

Visiting the heavens in Toronto

When I was six we stayed in my aunt's apartment
in the sky in Toronto, closer to heaven, jewels
of light tugged towards the horizon, headlights
like candy from her balcony. When I couldn't unlock
what kept me from jumping I threw up. Fear
of heights is sane. We aren't designed to fly. I was
unsure of this—having decided that
when I grew up I wanted wings. So now
my home is dangerous, 32 floors in the air.
What if at night I scale the railing
to feel free? They would call it suicide,
my lack of wings.

Antony Gormley is a hypocrite

but cut him some slack—he bit his silhouette
out of 8,640 slices of white bread and that's a lot
of work. He made *Bed* in 1981, the year my brother
emerged from my mother. By the year Dad walked out
the art had begun to deteriorate. He claims the piece
is about the inevitable destruction of matter,
transformation by consumption—

progression from solid to liquid to air. Mom
was less when Dad left. First, she cried
into her wrist, then she flew to another province,
converted her life. Solid to liquid to air. One person
can consume another. Gormley's art was moulding
so he agreed to dip it in wax, seal it from the inevitable—
it seemed like a good idea at the time.

The *Boogie Woogies* are on their last legs

At the MoMA they have the microscopes out
because something important is about to die.
Contemporary art is deteriorating, not withstanding
the test of time. Oh, not the ideas, but the proof—
Mondrian's last dance, 600 squares, the music
of Manhattan. It was the last thing he made,
his last attempt at pure abstraction.
Mondrian started a movement

with plastic paint. He wanted to
come so close to the truth he could turn
everything from it.

But the *Boogie Woogies* are going to disappear

Perhaps the highest form of abstraction
is disappearance. When the *Boogie Woogies*
are gone, we'll be left with the idea. They say
these are his masterpieces though they are
incomplete. So when we say *masterpiece*,
we mean his life which also, I think, is
unfinished. Mondrian died of pneumonia.
Before his death he radically altered
the *Victory Boogie Woogie,* bent over it

with coloured tape, coughed. Acrylic becomes brittle
with time, like us. The Mondrians
are slowly degrading. There are two kinds
of conservation: *prevention* and *intervention* and this
compels me. I see these paintings and I see us
eating fibre and omega-3s, making incisions, colouring
our lips, swallowing pills as if it were ordinary—
but I suppose it is: the urge to paint, to dance
some sort of boogie woogie.

Four versions of Jacob

It's impossible to unknot what the artist
attempts. We gravitate to the all-night Jacobs
without knowing we're searching
for assurance. Rembrandt's angel
considers Jacob with love, nearly lust,
about to succumb, patient and tender,
one naked leg clutching. Doré's pair is pressed
in dance, Michael about to say *left foot here,*
take your partner, un, deux, trois. Delacroix,
unafraid of struggle, paints insistence
and muscle. But it is Leloir whom I believe,
the only one to paint the dim, faith. Art
is two legs astride the chasm
of infinity, the rapture
of occasional wings.

I expect Castro will be dead
by the time you read this poem

but for now, he's still speaking. Or rather—
writing. *I do what I can: I write,* he said this year,
and we're all waiting for his last words. By the time
you read this, you'll know what he said. Karl Marx
spoke last to his housekeeper. *Go on, get out,*
he said, *last words are for fools who haven't said enough.*
Years later, Pancho Villa begged, *don't let it end like this,*
tell them I said something. Revolutionaries use words

to change the world. Oscar Wilde died in an ugly room
and his last words are my favourite. Sitting on the toilet
in my in-laws' house I think of him, accosted by the wallpaper,
which seems to have withstood the test of time. My mother-in-law
says her son is creative because of that visual
assault: orange and gold and velvet. I close my eyes on the throne,
and pity the man I love. Is it what we do or what we say
that survives?

Either it goes, or I do, Wilde said
and expired. Let me know
what Castro says—

november
(the trick of two worlds)

George, the year you carved your howl

for the first time I heard keening at the moon.
We'd moved to Canada, made a home in the woods,
and that August wolves sang, throats uplifted
in their feral chord, the liner notes for empty lungs.
Twelve months later blue-eyed Freya wandered out.
Off-balance and just fixed, she strayed
through the boot room. Dad said she joined the wolves.
That afternoon I'd curled into her under the piano
while she licked her stitches, traced a finger
along her wound, marvelled at the constellation
of her belly, freckles cast on pastel skin.

And when finally I learned to glide
through the woods on white, ski tips ahead,
a wolf shadowed us, disappeared every time we turned.
I bent over the only evidence, soft prints in snow.
Dad said it was Freya, gone wild and shy. I looked
for a wisp of breath, proof of lungs in cold.
In Germany, my sister tells me, they've asked the wolves back,
but wolf makes people think *Fenrir*, red-hooded girls,
and the woodcutters show up with guns.
Even if she had slipped out of her collar
domesticity isn't easily shaken. Raccoons,
they say, are the only ones who've learned
the trick of two worlds.

Mom rescued Alex Colville from the library

and we took him home, tattered and torn. A librarian
had taken scissors to him, removed the nakedness,
left the guns. Mom gathered up the loose pages,
carefully taped the women back in. *Violence,* she said
against love. I didn't know what she meant. Truth
lies in juxtaposition. *Painting occurs,* Alex says,
when I think of two disparate elements. That night
I opened *Tragic Landscape* on my lap and got lost
in the folds of cow beyond the soldier, still grazing,
as though death had taken nothing. I knew the man
was dead, but I searched the painting for a sign he was

sleeping. Later that year I was censored too, by Mrs. Milling,
who took my drawing of Adam and Eve and hid it
in her desk. She said I had made them too naked. Nakedness
makes us afraid. Imagine my mother hadn't
stitched up the book, imagine just *Pacific* and *Bodies
in a Grave, Belsen.* I spent the evening thinking
about guns, women in bathtubs, artists at war. What makes
something indecent is not skin but scissors.
This morning I tried to buy *The Art of Alex Colville,*
but it was too expensive. Tomorrow I'll try eBay,
perhaps someone doesn't know what it's worth.

I learned about guns from Alex Colville

When I was twelve Dad put a gun in my hands.
It wasn't the first time I'd held a weapon. We made
bows and arrows from saplings. But this time
it had heft because I knew what it was for.
I went inside and opened Colville, the book
with the binocular picture, the woman
who looked past me each time I went inside
for juice. Now I know what I was looking for—
Pacific, ironed pants, the weapon. Alex

has been accused of *emotional sterility*
but a woman with a revolver looking
for a midnight snack, anyone who tries to paint
the arc of wings, a hunting dog, has heart. Alex
left a message for me in *Prince Edward Island, Infantry
Near Nijmegen.* Guns
always say something.

Alex won't be here forever

i.

so I want to believe in heaven. Yann Martel
says we need to believe, that faith is vital,
but I'm afraid. I find bliss here and there
and on the beach with Alex, between the covers
of *The Facts Behind the Helsinki Roccamatios*—
but it's not enough. Alex says *you spend
your whole life telling people what it's like to be
alive.* I saw *Horse and Train* in Hamilton,
or at least it saw me, nickered. Alex visited
to calm us when we got nervous. Have you
rubbed a horse's neck when it's run out,
throbbing with terror? The city has forgotten
how to do this so Alex remembers for us,
rubs us down. We thought his horse had
shifted, grown darker, but it was just us,
loose in our feet. He reassured the conservator:
metaphysical darkness is difficult to gauge.

ii.

I don't want to die because emptiness frightens me,
but not nearly as much as nothing to fill. Alex
is an old man. Eventuality will claim him and I haven't
had the chance to shake his hand, tell him *Woman, Dog
and Canoe* prepared me for the river Styx.
That's how I'm leaving: upriver with a black dog.
Elizabeth I spent her last days on a pile of pillows,
said *all my possessions for a moment of time.* Which moment,
Alex, would you choose?

Misquoting Albert Einstein

i.

If Einstein said it, it would be true. That's why
he's misquoted, used for proof and we spar
on YouTube. Moonlighting prophets forecast
the end of the world, but that's old news. Everything
comes to a close even a good book. I thought
I wouldn't get to the end of *One Hundred Years
of Solitude* but I paddled to the last line:
*because races condemned to one hundred years
of solitude did not have a second opportunity
on earth.* Another theory of relativity. Einstein
didn't say our existence depends on honeybees, though
some are pinning it to him. I have no illusions
of understanding Marquez. In fact, I pressed through
his epic in a fog. But I like it
not knowing—

ii.

and knowing that if I spoke Spanish my world would be
different. Even if Einstein didn't say it honeybees are a substance,
heavy and sweet and without them some part of us would die.
In my first year of university my professor gave us Benjamin,
Barthes, Arendt. *Don't try to understand it now,* he said. I'm waiting
to understand solitude, the disappearance of bees, love
in the time of cholera. I found a reference to a sound bite
online: Berlin 1929—a poet and journalist (George
Sylvester Viereck, if you're interested) asks Einstein
how he accounts for his discoveries. *Through intuition
or inspiration? Both,* replies the genius, *I sometimes feel
I am right but I do not know it.* Einstein had faith
in imagination. *Imagination encircles the world,* I think
he said. The world is safe with Gabriel at the helm,
Einstein translating.

Clover sickness and the disappearance of bees

In grade ten I learned about *Catch-22s* and *slippery
slopes*. I read that honeybees are disappearing
because clover is in decline, that clover is disappearing
because honeybees are in decline. The paradox
is not as contradictory as it seems. We put the dog down
last year (*Honey*, because of her disposition, light
and sweet) for mercy. My brother was keeping her happy
by hot-boxing the car to soothe her joints. In Holland

they let the elderly die when they're ready. Mr. K.
said that was a slippery slope, and I imagined Oma
sliding off a dyke into the North Sea when her time came.
Clover sickness is a mystery. We just know that something's
wrong. There's no contradiction in what we did
when the dog died. Mom cried because I did, and I cried
because she did. Sorrow is always paradoxical, has something
to do with the disappearance of honey.

In my mother's house when we said sorry

we had to mean it which wasn't always
easy. On the last day of my brother's eighth year
I put the fear of God in him. I told him he was dying—
every second you are getting closer to your death
I said. *You will never be eight again.* The next morning
when Mom sang he wailed. When she found out
why, she made me read from James, as usual. *Your tongue,*
she said, *is a fire.* I sat at the table in shame. I read
about my tongue, a lick of evil. It would

set me alight. In my mother's house there was ritual—
I'm sorry, I said. *And what does that mean?* she
asked. *I'll try not to do it again,* I said. My brother
had to forgive me because those were the rules. Imperfect
contrition, also called attrition, is saying sorry for sorrow
of soul, fear of damnation. My brother hugged me
and wiped his nose in his sweatshirt. *I don't want to
forgive you,* he said, but he had no choice.

I get the email too—

the one we got this morning about getting bigger
to *satisfy the ladies.* The two of us hit *delete*—
it's not that there's anyone who doesn't
believe we're all connected, but sometimes
it's good to remind ourselves. Ten years ago,
on Laburnum Street, someone put a sign on the lavender:
don't rub too much please. All of us had been
pinching for pleasure, collectively snuffing beauty
by taking away the smell of it.

I spent the morning extracting dog hair
from my keyboard with a piece of paper.
The dog died last year but there she was,
under *ctrl* and *shift* with bread crumbs and fluff.

Last night Gigi asked if I'd written Caroline
into a poem yet. And now I've put her between *space*
and *enter* and I'm thinking of the way she touches things,
concerned not to leave prints, but leaving them
the way lavender and memory do. I go home thinking
about her hands, the length of them, their fine bones,
her porcelain neck, the way she changes a room
by being in it, like all of us,
and not like anyone else I know.

At 4 a.m. I lifted Timothy from my nightstand,

took him to the bath, lingered on the author's photo,
his soft white hair and I imagined him bent, writing.
He was my neighbour before I recognized his existence.
It's possible that when I was twelve he stood in front of me
at Canadian Tire with an extension cord. Now
I'm naked with him in the dark and looking

for some kind of light. I feel like I see him now
(because this is how we love our writers: we think
they've hidden themselves between the lines.
We think they know us because they love us).
Dad took me to Cannington to visit an illegal zoo,
a crazy man who owned a Siberian tiger
that believed a wolf was its mother. And now
I wonder, did Timothy see my tiger too? I want
to know how it is that he lives after he's died, an open novel
above my hot bath. Is this immortality or just an idea
in the early hours, that he tilted in my direction
before I knew he was there.

The most beautiful things I've seen in October

i.

My family, before the attrition, canoed—
all five of us in one long cedar strip. Dad
built it with love, the way you build a family,
and my brother, the only one without a paddle,
sat in the middle on an extra life jacket,
with a Zeller's fishing rod, a sandwich, claiming
he would catch the biggest bass. My sister and I
thought we were paddling, while in fact we were
feeling useful. It was my mother at the bow, pulling
us through Opeongo—the way, since then, she's
pulled us through everything. Dad, at the stern,
made sure to cut the waves *just so.* You have to
cross the lake to get inside. Beyond the portages,
there's peace—our aim, to get away, to be

ii.

alone in October. But the first night we stayed
on Bates Island—Opeongo was forceful that day—
and our arms were tired. In the morning we did the first
portage, *left civilization*, as Dad liked to say, his prelude
to talking about the Voyageurs, singing *en roulant ma boule,
roulette*. Algonquin was on fire that weekend, and we
saw a moose browsing, all five of us held our breath
for the soft chewing, to hear water fall from his mouth,
the suction of feet as he disappeared into the forest.
Even though Dad sold the canoe, and left the four of us
stranded without someone at the stern, that day was
lovely—I looked at a moose through the triangle of his arm
steadying the boat with a paddle, wiggling his eyebrows
at me, nothing but love and maples. That month

iii.

Carola Frehe and Raymond Jakubauskas died
on Bates Island. A black bear interrupted them
preparing ground beef. Raymond took a crack
with a paddle to save Carola, but failed. The bear
was autopsied—he killed them for *no reason*. No
disease or provocation. Some things are inexplicable—
the way autumn feels, a leaf on Opeongo, my Dad
abandoning us, despite October. Have you ever noticed
the way a cellist gets lost in the music? The way lips
express the efforts of the heart. We're vulnerable
like that, in the presence of moose and music
and our fathers, whom we love with a nakedness
no matter what they've done, or might.

It-is-having-a-long-neck

i.

in Cayuga, the translation of giraffe. Languages
are disappearing and how you feel
is up to you. When Oma buys bread and grapes
the cashier asks her where she's from. Oma
hates the question, a reminder that she's failed
at shedding her Netherlands. *I've been here
forty years* she groans and turns the key. She's proud
of who she is, but she wants people to know
this is her home. I love the Dutch in her syllables,
a reminder of where I come from. Location
isn't always geographic. I've peeked

ii.

at Cree, Haida, glottal stops. Dutch has a word
that can't be translated, *gezellig.* Some will tell you
one word encompasses an entire nation. My Oma
photographing a giraffe, buying us ice cream,
doling out ham and pea soup Sundays, that was
gezellig—what happens when you're with
the people you love, in the place you want to be.
I searched the obituaries of *The Economist.* Marie
Smith is dead. Her real name is another word
I can't pronounce, *Udachkuqax*a'a'ch:*

iii.

her name means *a sound that calls people from afar.*
Attrition, when your language leaves you. Loneliness,
when you're the last one left: *ongezellig.* Marie
wanted to be a pilot when she was little. When she
died Eyak died too. Ovide Mercredi addressed
an audience after Oka, because everything
was at stake. *I live different from you,* he said,
*not that I hate you but because I like the way we live
ourselves, as people.* My Oma does some inexplicable
things. She has a carpet on her coffee table,
eats candied salt. Marie Smith, according to the
magazine, knew what the death of Eyak meant.
She said it was *the not-to-be-imagined
disappearance of the world.*

I'm afraid, and it's not just
the disappearance of bees

i.

it's because I don't want to die, not just because
dying means no more avocados, reading
Margaret Atwood in the bath, deciding
when the flowers are too wilted, folding
laundry. I don't want to die because I love
the plant on the balcony shivering 32 stories
from the ground, vacuuming pennies. I'm only
starting to figure out how to write what I feel, how to
tell you why I love *Hair pursued by two planets*

and *Poppyseed Cake: Glazed for Calypso.* I wrote
a letter to Alex Colville, imploring him not to die because
they found Ernesto Che Guevara's body, missing
two hands. Sartre said Che was *the most complete human
being of our age* even without his hands. *The true
revolutionary*, Che said, *is guided by a great feeling
of love.* This has something to do with Alex Colville
and bees but I haven't figured it out yet and I think
I'm going to run out of time.

ii.

I'm not convinced of *ashes to ashes,* and all that
jazz. I don't want to be dust, even though the metaphor
is lovely. I don't want to return, in any state, because
I don't want to come back. I want to stay
long enough to find out what happens, to make amends
with my father, heaven and here. I want to understand
how one person can cut off the hands of another, how one bird
in the right moment can change your mind. You're
going to tell me I'm young, because I am. I'm too young

to be thinking about dying—but all the time
in the world is not enough. I've just realized
how insignificant I am, what it means to find a little
brown bat, dead from expansion. I've only just begun
to feel. By the time I'm 42, they say half of the birds,
the languages of the world, will be extinct. It will take
more than my lifetime to translate that, get it
down. I don't know how

iii.

Sartre said it in French, but in English *every existing thing
is born without reason, prolongs itself out of weakness,
and dies by chance.* A bird flew into the window
and I knew it was my fault—for having a window, wanting
to see the mountains. In my hands it kept breathing,
its heart the sound of my nephew in the morning, rushing
to his mother, my sister. It snapped on the glass, expired

because it had no choice and I had no place
to bury it. I thought about putting it in the garburator
with the coffee grinds and bread crumbs because
I live in a hive with no backyard. It couldn't be *dust
to dust* because I'm surrounded by concrete and glass. So
I had to put it in the compactor and there was something
awful about that, its body in a plastic bag, the smell
of fruit, a tossed diaper. There's another thing Sartre said,
that *God is the solitude of man.*

iv.

I've only started to learn about dinosaurs, to find my way
around the vegetable aisle. I'm sure there are thousands
of ways to say *I'm sorry, I love you,* and *I don't know*—
but all I get is one sip of that fine syrah, a few languages.
I don't think I'm going to learn Spanish, master
sourdough, glass-blowing. The bacteria in the Precambrian
Shield are over two billion years old and yesterday the president
bailed out the banks with 700 billion. Numbers will be
the last thing I understand before I die. Imagine, the earth
is only four and a half billion, give or take. I checked the net

and found out trilliums grow on the Canadian Shield.
The biggest things are explained by the smallest things. Ants
nibble on trilliums, and when they're done throw away
the most important part, the seed. When I was little
I had a doll *Frosta,* who had the ability to create ice
at will. I left her outside one winter and found her in June—
squirrels had eaten her breasts, her face, the softest parts
of her body. Just now, I discovered online,
she comes from *Etheria,* a fictional place—which means
despite not really existing at all, I managed to love her.

The day Mom failed to rescue Icarus
from the Dutch

i.

The Dutch are famous for coffee houses, red-fringed
parlours and tulips. We've got Rembrandt and
the Reformation and after the war we tucked *de Reformatie*
into our sleeves, bulbs in suitcases, and left
the Rijksmuseum behind. My people travelled light
in the 40s and 50s—carried seeds to the Golden
Horseshoe and Edmonton. On this side of the water
we emptied our pockets, planted schools and potatoes,
apples. I went to a CRC school (not to be confused with
CCR) and I was a *Calvinette* in the church basement,
a lineup of little girls in white scarves, aspiring
to *do justice, to love mercy, and to walk humbly
with our God.* I was expected to *love suffering*—
the cornerstone of being human, reformed. Mom
was too late to rescue Icarus—

ii.

she found him fluttering to the garbage. Armed
with X-acto knives, the PTA was removing the Greeks
from our readers. Phaeton was on the floor with his chariot
and wood nymphs, amber tears and Helios. *These men,*
the women said, *are trying to fly to the wrong God.* Mom
covered her mouth, left the room. By the time I sprouted
my own apples, my faith was a *bad moon arising, trouble
on the way.* Sometimes immigrants leave things behind,
travel too light, forget to shoulder
the art of history.

The dessert comes after the ham

Boterkoek tastes better than its translation, butter-cake,
and the first time I translated *ollie bollen* into English
I understood words have nothing to do with taste.
Laid bare in another language they mean nothing,
oil balls. When Oma made chocolate chip cookies
we asked her for *bolletjes,* dough rolled in her white hand,
popped into our mouths and they tasted like love,
though Google translate will tell you the word
is *bullet, small bun.* Once, after boterkoek

my brother bit me—this was before
illness and tablets stole Oma's clarinet, her desire
for Mozart and ham. She wiped her hands
on her apron and chased him under the organ
where she sank her teeth into his little arm. *Don't bite
your sister,* she said. Pain can be translated
because it's the only Esperanto. My brother
gazed at his arm, Oma's fresh moon dents. *Come,
have some ham, schaatje,* she said to him. Schaatje
means schaatje—there's no other word
for being small.

Out with a whimper

Oma didn't go to university. The war ended
and she huddled with her siblings in the belly
of a ship, arrived in Halifax, worked the soil.
But if you could have heard her crescendo
on the clarinet, seen her vacuuming with Amadeus
shaking the house. Opa had a heart attack
in the garage and she lifted him up, a kind of music—
the way the body does what it can't for love
out of necessity. She'd been trying to lose weight

when they diagnosed her with cancer
and in two months she was whittled. Opa
and Mozart kept her alive. All she wanted:
Agnus Dei and a photograph of one great swell
above her bed, a slow wave about to shore.
That was death as she imagined it, without words,
Mozart and Opa's hand.

The physical properties of light

Oma, in a moment of clarity, confided in my mother—
old age feels so sudden. She told me once
she hated getting old—*People don't move out of my way
anymore, I have to open my own doors.* Men stopped
noticing her sweep of black hair because
it had grown white. After too many days in the sun
we evaporate, the colour leaves our bodies.
Alex Colville says he wants his art to be permanent
which means he wants it to outlast him. Art
is a brush with immortality, an attempt to escape
our fugitivity. They say the universe began

in a burst of light and *God saw that the light was good
and he separated it from the darkness.* That was the first day
and every day after that we've been finding ways
to let the light in. Mom opens the blinds in Oma's
room, I light a candle beside the bed. All of us create
friction with our bodies to remember
how the universe began, small explosions
in dim rooms, the only way to separate ourselves
from night. But it's light that ruins paintings
so the only way to preserve anything is to hide it,
trap Mondrian in argon under glass
in the basement without us.

Some people sit behind a curtain
to talk to the Lord

and I sit behind paper, before paper, after paper.
You cannot trust a poem. A poem is a metaphor
and a metaphor is a lie. Let me show you, let me
scribble *I am paper* in this poem. If you believe me
you can decide if I will burn or if I am a house
for Atticus or Scout. I may be full sails, an envelope
for the future. I can hoist the Vitruvian Man and I may,
at any moment, fold myself into an impossible crane.
I can carry my own blue sky. The strongest things
are the weakest things, the flammable words, the ache
for God, immortality. I can make a thousand suns
without igniting anything. You know what paper is—
it's proof, proof that one person wants to be heard,
proof that some things should last forever, that love
should be recorded, that beauty is urgent. Paper is
the only way I can talk to God and honeybees
and the Mt. Glorious torrent frog, all the wings
I want to believe in but cannot. I sit behind paper
to talk to the Lord, to confess to love,
to detonate.

december
(a bowl of strawberries in an empty room)

I wonder if I'll be like Georgia, rummaging

solitary in the garden, swept by black mesa,
red hills, sweet green shoots and used bones.
I don't know if I can fail to teach new legs
how to pedal, spoon raspberries into a perfect mouth,
curl into a soft corner with *Frog and Toad*
or *this little piggy went home.* I don't know if I can
face the emptiness of my body. Will you
bring this poem to my deathbed,

say *why didn't you have children?* And what
will I tell you? I chose sweet peas and the harmattan,
blue nights and red wine, soft cheese, a quiet studio, love
in other bundles. Will I lament not teaching small feet
to propel a bicycle? Georgia said of the hills she loved:
they're almost painted for you, you'd think until you try.
What will fit into me exactly?

**I was painting a door
when my sweetheart's drained face**

phone in hand like a limp mouse, said
call your sister, the baby—and then—
is dead. The universe hit the door and
vanished. I found a bag, wrapped my paintbrush
and set it on the floor. And then I called
through cable across dormant Saskatchewan,
graffiti on the granite shield. *I love you,* I said

and tried not to weep. And then details:

*I baked cookies Friday, she stopped moving,
her name is Keira Jo.* For the last several months
I'd probed for the secret name of the girl
but now the name premature, and the little one
late. *Yesterday,* Rachel said, *she was fine.*
She was spinning in infinity, pressing
her soles against my sister who wonders
if she was trying to kick her way out, if she
was looking for the door with her heels,
if she could have done anything.

I thought the sky would be different

after Keira Jo died but when I faced the canvas
brush wet with everything my heart couldn't
carry it was blue, brilliant bright. It was
Saskatchewan this summer, the sun
so much we stopped to watch wheat curve
along the horizon. Today I painted the sky I want
and not the one I carry. I don't want that
small face in a white casket, slight lid, naked
maples quaking, Rachel's face framed
by a pale blue toque, all of us entombed

by December, blowing white, without mittens,
Dad's ears cherry red. I put a hand in Josh's
so he could carry me, my small hand in his big one,
white gull in a white sky. We carry each other
without lifting—by sudden gusts of love.
The miracle of being human, isn't it? Briefly,
Keira Jo carried Rachel, by the lift of the idea of her.
Rachel carried the future for nine months
and then let go. The sky is indifferent
but offers everything: hope and birds, light
on curves so even sorrow has a rim.

Mom and I, sunk on the brown couch,

held the number in our cheeks—$165,
winter fee—the price of dying in December.
What does that mean? We stared into our empty
mugs. That number was inadequate, the idea
that loss can be calculated, that it
has something, anything to do
with a backhoe. *It's more difficult*

to dig a grave when the ground is frozen,
we were told. August at least
could have offered eggplants in the garden,
purple, some pleasant row to lie in afterwards,
warm comfort of knowing winter could approach
slowly—start with her fingers, end in her chest.
But now Keira Jo won't thaw until spring. She won't
begin to disappear until April.

A bowl of strawberries in an empty room

i.

Rachel insisted Keira Jo be swaddled, not clothed.
She's not a doll, she said. And besides
there are rituals reserved for mothers. The gentle
first tug of naked arms through cotton, white socks
on new feet. She didn't want her daughter dressed
the first time by a mortician, lovingly or by rote. *It was,*
Rachel said, *the most terrifying moment of my life*—
preparing to hold her dead girl, *a pixie,*
she said, *perfect.* When I stooped over the box

Keira Jo was wearing a yellow toque, swaddled
in white, an almost-child. Small red face, perfect
lips. Plutarch, in *Moralia,* wrote *not to be born is best
of all, and death better than life,* but the wisdom
of Silenus is stilled by one small mouth at the breast,
a tiny heart—that sparrow, Rachel's thumb
clutched by a small pink hand, any flutter
however small.

ii.

so red has changed, it used to be Georgia's
poppies, the upward scatter of gladiolas
in a room. But now it is three long stems
arranged on a white casket, a box too small
for flowers, the universe. We knelt in snow
far away from prayer, offered a stem
already dead. Our red hands were an illusion

of summer, perhaps the truth of it. Temporal,
fugitive red, we tried to balance it on a box
of darkness. I'd never liked roses, but now
one saved stem hangs in the laundry room
at my sister's, like Keira Jo upside down
in the dark, waiting for her mother
to hold the bloom in her hands
when she's ready.

iii.

I'd never loved Rachel so much as that moment
in Keira Jo's vacant room, surrounded by empty
shirts, small striped socks. Rachel, wrapped in
a white duvet, saying only *I wanted her, I wanted
her so badly.* And I kneeled before her, wept
into her lap—my sister, like her daughter, delicate
and bloodshot. Beauty, love, are inexplicable. I was
at Rachel's knee, flushed with sorrow, a moose
on a dark highway. I remembered Freetown—
the two of us girls making castles
at the edge of the world.

iv.

Our mother says *amendment*—the sudden berry
inside me, small and red and waiting. It's an accident
and I feel like Judas, sewing after the collapse
of Keira Jo whom I want to honour
by a crater in the heart, the womb.

v.

And just then a bowl of strawberries
changed my mind, red shining off the sides
of a steel bowl and that smell of June
in the dark. Cleaning the windows, I decided
to plant oregano and butter-leaf 32 floors from the ground,
a container garden, absurd as carrying a person
below the heart, beneath the ribs, letting
it grow until it spills, presses for more
room, leaps over the rim, that fiery edge
between mother and world. I do want amendment,
a garden in the air. A world without
Keira Jo.

I told my first stranger I was pregnant,

i.

a cashier in red. And on the couch today
reading *Headhunter* finally after putting it off
for years, I felt my skin grow taut. Beached
on the couch I recognized I love libraries
but hate library books, orange grease
on the pages from some man's burrito,
the thought of his sweat seeping into the pages,
my book perched on his naked belly. Most of all
I'm loathe to know that what I'm reading isn't mine.
Someone else guffawed where I did, nodded
in pleasure at the thought of Kurtz, escaped
from *Heart of Darkness*. Motherhood
is like that, and love: we want to own—

ii.

be the first one suspended by miracle.
Since *The Piano Man's Daughter* I've had it
out for Findley, always killing the characters
I love most. But I can't help slipping in again,
having faith—in him and, of course, that book
of ours, life between the covers of love and
death, full of red and people I'll never meet,
(even the one who spilled bean juice
on the paragraph about the stillborn, the jar).

This is the moment I realize
the ones we love disappear, afloat
in sorrow, inexplicably shelved.

january
(it's impossible to put my finger on that bird)

**The first movement
(adagio with seabirds, perhaps the Beck's petrel—
thought to be extinct but assumed alive)**

i.

The first thing to die was my family—
there was no way to clutch that bird,
bury it, mourn its loss. My family failed
without failing. The maples turned
and then Dad did. There was an unexpected
chasm, one we still attempt to soar. Love
is always impossible though paradoxically
it's the impulse that makes everything possible.
That was the first time the world ended, Dad
sobbing, out of love, and me cross-legged
with Colville on my lap,

ii.

and I understood for the first time transformation,
the way Alex's bird inexplicably changed
when Mom was cast off. That painting,
my world, was no longer about flight.
I rediscovered the painting of the *soldier*
and the girl. Until that moment I thought
it was reunion, love—and then I realized
he was leaving. I wanted to find the instant
Dad quit needing us, thought if I knew I might
have done what crows do, distracted threat
with swooping. Did we end when love did,
or when Dad made the declaration, that terrible
warble in the throat? The next day

iii.

Oma washed the windows, dragged vinegar
and newspaper along the glass and wept. Cedars
and maples swayed out front, Mom's kitchen silent
behind her. There was nothing Oma could do
for her girl despite having hoisted her by the armpits,
having taught her to brush her teeth, use a fork, shuck.
But now, she said, *there is no lifting,* only a dirty paper
yellowed with woodsmoke. She could only
make the view a little easier.

The second movement
(allegro with finches,
most likely yellow in great number)

iv.

At 5:20 my mother called and hung up,
realizing that it was too early, that it wasn't
light yet on my side of the world. Oma lived
three hours longer in BC because
I didn't know. For the first time the riddle
made sense: Oma in the forest still standing
until I, the last one to acknowledge her death,
let her fall to some kind of silent music,
a lonely rustle, when the phone rang
for the second time.

The third movement
(to 31 minutes and 19 seconds of Marais la Nuit,
Neko's spring peepers)

v.

I spent the day Oma died under scrutiny.
I told the doctor I walk every day
though I didn't tell her about the owl in the hemlock,
that I go to the forest to check if it's still there—
the forest, me, nameless brown birds
darting underbrush, disturbing nothing
but silence. She searched for a heartbeat,
said it might be hiding under my pelvic bone
and I thought what an odd and wonderful place
for the heart, having felt my own there
from time to time.

vi.

Two days later a technician scattered sound
under the shelf of my pelvis, told me the fluttering
ceased weeks ago. *How is it,* I asked my pillow,
that I carried the dead without knowing? I tell myself
it was only a berry, though I know now nothing
is only anything. Was Keira Jo quiet before Rachel
felt her silence? Did Oma die when she yielded,
stopped playing—or was it when Opa knelt
at her tomb, said *goodbye my girl,*
let her go?

vii.

I called Mom and I had no language
to describe what had ceased
to flicker, never kicked or fallen,
died before I believed its existence.
It had, of course, been loved—the only proof
of existence, that message in the sky Auden
transcribed—

a silent piano, doves, the reason
we hold each other in the dark,
scatter sound.

viii.

Oma told Opa she wanted to wear
her grey dress to the fireworks this spring
but spring will arrive without her. Now
I think *I must paint* but I've forgotten how
or why. I sift and sift for a precise moment
as if exactitude might offer insight.
I wonder how long I carried someone

who wasn't, marvelled
at the tattoo my mother gave me, the cave
of my navel—that rope in the dark. We begin
with explosion but death is another kettle, inexact,
slow no matter how sudden. The mountains settled
on the horizon this morning, proof
of something.

february
(browsing *frog and toad* together)

Browsing *Frog and Toad* together

i.

Mom used to read to us *Frog and Toad*—
she'd take her violin into the dark, sing
to the seeds in the night, implore little rows
to push up, out. Every spring moose browse
new buds and last month, beached
on the couch, I browsed cashews and Findley,
said to the arch of my belly—*now, seed,*
start growing, beseeched the regular miracle.
Of course sometimes nothing pushes up
out of darkness—

ii.

so I watched a movie about replanting mangroves,
another way to save the planet. A team of helicopter
pilots fired seed pods into the beach. The conditions,
they say, were perfect. Well—inexplicably nothing
became of the beginning. Life is precarious
because frog and toad together on Mom's lap isn't
ordinary. A female moose browses with her calf
only three weeks after emerging from the dark
and before I was born Mom balanced novels
on the arc of me, pages turning, a music
I was learning to love—

but—we begin books we don't finish, a moose
gives birth to blood in a curve of snow. We play
violins in the dark and I have to remember
it isn't for nothing even if it is.

I visited an online forum, Kathy and Ottawa

back and forth about tomatoes and chard.
Ottawa laments the *failure of her window-*
box romas and Kathy says she's *run out*
of summer. Do you think, they to and fro,
there was enough light? Rachel refused
an autopsy because she knew operating light
wouldn't answer her only steel question,
not *how* or *how come*, but *dear-God-why?*

Tossing at night we rummage our hollows
for fault lines. Mothers whose beginnings
are flushed ferret themselves. I worry I fissured
because of Jägermeister on the 25th, because
my sweetheart took me skiing
with a bowl of strawberries in my jacket.
I lie awake, imagine them in snow, crushed
under the weight of me. Prying me open,
the doctor said *nature corrects itself*
out of necessity and today gulls, tossed
in the grey, offered flight, another necessity,
though not mine—

I wrote about fading Mondrians
(and it was after that)

I wonder if it's my fault. I left my bike outside
all winter without riding it. Come spring
I didn't fix it. I should have asked for help
but not knowing how I hauled it to the curb
for someone to steal, make it work, take hope
in the broken thing—

a seat-less bicycle leaning against Dad's hayloft,
too small to ride though I'm grinding gears
to make it fly.

Fire, earth, water, bicycle

i.

Wanting salamander and other kinds of fire

I'm not water despite the 90 percent I'm told
and salamanders are the real phoenixes—lose
what they need and grow it back. The amphibian
isn't destroyed by winter, curls into the cold, drops tail
when the curious enemy gets too close. I only wish
I could have dropped something when the predator
loomed, threatened to steal that thing I thought
was part of me. I keep looking for it under the bed,
loose in the bathroom drawer, a misplaced
bobby pin. What I don't say is how much I want
to grow it back, small limb, a part of me I didn't know
I needed.

ii.

Searching the sweet peas for what I've lost

Some things are too small to see
except through the lens of love. What I carried
was somewhere to land. It was minute
but changed the world. When Rachel lost Keira Jo
she said she understood the story
of Solomon's whores, willing to trade the dead
for the living. I lost something that nearly existed
but Rachel was full bloom. *Earth*, I whispered to her,
both of us swollen with emptiness, *somewhere
to plant our feet but not the whole head-to-toe
however small.* How do you bury someone
who doesn't exist?

iii.

One last swim and the curse of Undine

Before Rachel's baby died, she swam—
and we delighted at the pool of her, infant in the eddy
of mother, mother weightless in water. I visited
the aquarium while I was hollowing. The dolphin
is a riddle, having solved the curse we can't.
Some of us expire in sleep. *Undine's curse* they call it,
the inability to breathe involuntarily. The dolphin
takes turns, one half of its brain sleeping
while the other swims. I want
to lullaby sorrow, still
the tired half.

iv.

My bicycle and other modes of flight

We come up gasping from sorrow. The only answer
is breath. There are whales that scrape the ocean floor
and dive upwards. The emperor penguin plunges
half a kilometre to get what he needs. When I was
small I believed in heaven, some sort of membrane
between earth and perfection. We spend our lives
coming up for air, searching for krill, small creatures
that give us a reason to continue. I want to fly—
not to paradise to visit the impossible—but on my bicycle
I want to break the barrier between sorrow
and joy.

march
(a denouement with bicycles)

Oma's at the sink, though I'm told

she's in the ground. Last month I pressed
my hands on my belly. *I think*, I said, *I'll give birth
to a hero*. The impulse

is gone, though part
remains, and Keira Jo's heel-prints
engrave the inside of Rachel. Oma
left Mozart and the noise of cutlery
in the rooms she graced.

The sand tiger shark is tougher than me

i.

which comes as a surprise to no one.
By now you know I'm tugged by the fugitive
line of duck on water, the generous drag
of butter on bread, pedaling. My survival
instinct is awry. I'm reading *Floating in My
Mother's Palm* because I believe tenderness
and loss are the slag of love, that the dead
tell us how to live. I realized this morning
why I love runts. It's self-pity and it's lovely,
how vulnerable we are. On the other hand,
sand tiger sharks have two chambers in the womb
to prevent one pup from eating the other.
This morning

ii.

on YouTube, a young albatross was sharked
from the surface and because I'm composed
of carbon and softness, I wonder which sailor
will lose hope tomorrow, robbed of his omen.
I am hollowed out and glancing
to the sky for some place to land. Even warm
and adrift in our mothers' rooms
we live in a dangerous curve. What is it
the dead are trying to tell us? Keira Jo is proof
that love and suffering are two rooms
in the same chamber, but the shark pup
exits jaws open with no need of its mother—

There's an albino pigeon
that lands from time to time

beside my chained-up bicycle. It sets me to wondering,
not the way I wonder about other pigeons, emerald-ringed,
or the way I soften walking under a bridge, swallowed
by the whirring of all those grey breasts. This bird
is a kind of light but does it know? I got lost this morning
googling the *Great Pacific Garbage Patch*. I cascaded
through photos of albatrosses, open cadavers of young ones
fed fragments of flip-flops, turquoise barrettes, bottle caps
by their mothers. When we don't understand something
we look for complicated answers. We say *the albatross
can't discern between the flash of food and the gleam
of plastic* but perhaps she can't believe something caustic
is carried by ocean swells. Maybe she carefully selects

red caps, round things, objects that whistle. I was told
Melanesia was found by the lost, learned later of catamarans,
a people so settled on water they could read its ridges,
so it wasn't Medusa's raft that washed up on the sand.
I am imagining a historian standing in a Hopi house
believing it was built for war. I try to understand
him erasing the Grand Canyon to see enemies flinging dust.
And here, at my desk, I'm trying to understand why I love
the albino pigeon. Do I love her because she's different, because
I want to know if the others can see the way she shines? I realize
it's absurd to believe all the other pigeons are blind.

                         It's simpler to imagine
they are startled by her, that she knows the darkest thing
about her is her shadow. It's simpler to believe in beauty,
that in most instances beauty is why we sail and build houses
and navigate by a white pigeon.

They dissected the bullfrog
and revealed a belly full

of small alligators. We make incisions
in search of clarity, simplicity. Instead we find
the natural order of the universe, our trajectory
towards chaos. Survival is always accidental,
ignited by one kind of poverty or another. Math
is beautiful and perplexing. Did you hear about the man
who sailed through the air, was stopped by a bridge?

He didn't intend to die—he expected to land,
a yellow parachute fluttering behind. Despite
the chaos of his ending, his catastrophe can be expressed
with flawless curves, perfect lines, parabolas.
Is it suicide to eat alligators for nourishment, to want
to fly, or is it the only response to the accident
of existence?

It's the small things that save us

Neko's *Middle Cyclone* came at just the right moment—
robins and frogs, the night chorus last track, proof
of strength in numbers, what it means to sing
together. Oma and Opa sang *By the Sea of Crystal*
to stave off hell, me and Mom on the phone,
naked in our bathtubs, giggling about something
inconsequential, Neko's piano orchestra,
a ragtag collection of rescued keys. It's not
our usefulness that makes us
matter, or makes us at all; it's who we are
in chorus. She sings *in the wintertime*
keep your feet warm, so I'm waiting
for spring peepers
with a hot water bottle.

The extraordinary feat of calling my mother

i.

It used to be our voices couldn't travel far—
we had to fold them into envelopes, rely
on our mother's memory of the sound of us,
saying *pass the salt, the pain is in my abdomen,
I can't sleep.* Our mothers unfolded us long after
we spoke—by a window, the garden. And then
we distilled our voices into telegraphs and cables
and now our connections are cellular—our voices
ride waves, the sound of me arrives at my mother's
through invisible circuitry so I can say

the pain is inexplicable, I can't sleep. She relies
on a recollection of me eight years old and afloat
in the tub, humming—traversing the inexplicable
passageways of love through sound. *Your hair,*
she tells me now, *was a halo around innocence.*
She offers what I can't see as some sort of balm,
an inversion of words and memory. *This is you,*
she says, as if it explains everything. Maybe
it does. There are

ii.

those who believe we are defined by the planets—
that my point of emergence occurred with solar
exactitude. I'm always surprised by affinity,
that I can find you with this lexis, that you might
locate me. Somewhere on the shore of this poem
I am made visible, I occur, I begin—a pinpoint. I am
a lonely goat, they say, *I crave recognition. Capricorn
is the opposite of Cancer.* I want to know what that means.

I've scoffed at astrology, but my phone call travels
invisible waves beyond the atmosphere to reach
my mother. Every night I'm moved by the planets,
assuaged. Luna says *call your mother,* moonlight
rides a different kind of pulse—an undulation capable
of carrying light, lifting something that's weightless.
So I want to know: which gesture carries sorrow, sparrows?
I say to my mother *I can't find my balance* and my
words bounce off heaven to reach her. Of course

iii.

I can't. I think I'm standing still but I'm spinning
in infinity. My voice finds her through the commotion:
the painting I'm negotiating, my glass of water.
Even my pancreas is whirling in search of alignment,
an organ I've never seen but believe in nonetheless
because my existence depends on it. Inside the inside
of me there are clusters of cells, small planets,
organs playing that I can't hear. My pancreas

houses one million islets of Langerhans, their total mass
weighs only one gram. My body proves a grain of rice
is the expression of the universe, faith is desire
for cellular affinity and hope is a solitary voice
in the cosmos. Of course I'm conflicted
by the sparrow on the sidewalk, a halo of blood
around its head, an open walnut. It died
because of me, because of our terrible velocity

iv.

towards bedlam. It collided with a moving window
on the King George, a highway named after
an extinct monarch. I took that bird home
without lifting it and I buried it in this poem. It begins
to exist now that it's dead, because of you and me
finding each other, proving every object that falls
makes a sound whether or not we know we exist:
the pat of this poem on your heart, the molecular orchestra
of my body pumping out music I can't hear,

even that tree we riddle over—the one that makes
an explosive descent despite our absence. Silence
is impossible—it's only that listening is so difficult.
Everything and nothing depends on you
and me. The ordinary is always astonishing: we,
strange to each other when I began, now sit intimately
before this poem spinning around the sun, our bodies
containing one million small islands, cellular arcs
with a trajectory towards chaos and our mothers
who will always know how to unfold us, no matter
the distance they must travel, or how.

notes

Four versions of Jacob: four paintings of the story of Jacob wrestling the angel. *Jacob Wrestling with the Angel*, Eugene Delacroix, 1857-1861 (Église Saint-Sulpice, Paris); *Jacob Wrestling with the Angel*, Gustave Doré, 1855 (Granger Collection, New York); *Jacob Wrestling with the Angel*, Alexander Louis Leloir, 1865 (Musée des Beaux-arts, Clermont-Ferrand, France); and *Jacob Struggles with the Angel*, Rembrandt van Rijn 1659 (Gemäldegalerie, Berlin).

George, the year you carved your howl: George A. Walker's woodcut *Howl* (1986), included in *The Wayzgoose '86 Anthology.* The woodcut is also in *The Inverted Line* (2000), published by the Porcupine's Quill. Raccoons, according to some sources, can return to the wild after being tamed.

Mom rescued Alex Colville from the library: *Tragic Landscape*, Alex Colville, 1945 (Beaverbrook Collection of War Art); *Pacific*, Alex Colville, 1967 (Private Collection); *Bodies in a Grave, Belsen*, Alex Colville, 1946 (Canadian War Museum). In a *Globe and Mail* interview, Colville is quoted as saying, "I do have a fear of chaos and a strong sense of the fragility of civilization."

I learned about guns from Alex Colville: *To Prince Edward Island*, Alex Colville, 1965 (National Gallery of Canada); *Infantry near Nijmegen, Holland*, Alex Colville, 1946 (Canadian War Museum). According to Library and Archives Canada, this painting has an alternate title: *Terrible Beauty, 1946.* It's a painting of the 3rd Canadian Infantry marching atop a dyke; the other painting mentioned in the poem is *Woman with Revolver*, Alex Colville, 1977 (Art Gallery of Nova Scotia). In 2005, this painting was vandalized (most likely with a paper clip or some other small, sharp object) while on exhibit at the Mendel Art

Gallery in Saskatoon. Kotyk, the collections manager for the Mendel, said "it was just a foolish person doing a foolish thing," as the piece is not controversial.

Alex won't be here forever: *The Facts Behind the Helsinki Roccamatios and Other Stories* is a collection of short stories by Yann Martel, first published as a paperback by Knopf Canada, 1993; *Horse and Train*, Alex Colville, 1954 (Art Gallery of Hamilton) was inspired by two lines from a Roy Campbell poem, "Dedication to Mary Campbell": "Against a regiment I oppose a brain / And a dark horse against an armored train"; *Woman, Dog and Canoe*, Alex Colville, 1982 (Art Gallery of Ontario).

Misquoting Albert Einstein: Einstein has been attributed with saying: "if the bee disappears from the surface of the earth, man would have no more than four years to live." This quote (while I was writing this book) was zipping around the web. The quote is most likely bogus. In fact, it seems to have originated 40 years after the death of the physicist.

It-is-having-a-long-neck: Eyak is an extinct Na-Dené language that was spoken in south-central Alaska. Marie Smith Jones (Udachkuqax*a'a'ch:) died January 21, 2008 at the age of 89 of natural causes. She was the last full-blooded Eyak, and the last speaker of her language. Udachkuqax*a'a'ch:, translated, means "to call people from afar." She was a vocal advocate for the preservation of indigenous languages.

I'm afraid, and it's not just the disappearance of bees: *Hair Pursued by Two Planets*, Joan Miró, 1968 (The Joan Miró Foundation, Barcelona, on loan from K.A.G. Gallery); *Poppyseed Cake, Glazed for Calypso*, Mary Pratt, 2002. According to a study conducted on a wind-farm in Alberta (published in *Current Biology*), wind-turbines are killing bats without touching them.

A localized drop in air-pressure caused by the whirling blades of the turbines causes the bats' lungs to burst. Their air sacs overexpand and their lungs fill with blood.

I wonder if I'll be like Georgia, rummaging: If you get the chance (before it disappears) check out the YouTube clip: http://www.youtube.com/watch?v=BYwKRVJaNEA

I told my first stranger I was pregnant: *Headhunter,* Timothy Findley, published by HarperCollins (1993); *The Piano Man's Daughter,* Timothy Findley, published by HarperCollins (1995).

The first movement: To date, only three of Beck's petrels have been found. In fact, the last dead specimen found is used for proof of its existence. We don't know where they breed, perhaps somewhere in the southern Bismarck Archipelago or southeast of New Guinea.

The third movement & It's the small things that save us: Neko is Neko Case. The album referred to is *Middle Cyclone,* released March 2009 by Anti-.

Browsing *Frog and Toad* together: *Frog and Toad Together* is a collection of children's stories written and illustrated by Arnold Lobel (1971, I Can Read). "The Garden" is a little story about Toad planting seeds and fearing they won't sprout. He coaxes them and in the end (spoiler alert) the seeds turn into plants.

The sand tiger shark is tougher than me: *Floating in My Mother's Palm* by Ursula Hegi, Simon & Schuster (1990). Two young sand tiger sharks are born every other year, one from each uterus. Each surviving embryo kills and eats the smaller embryos and feeds on unfertilized eggs during nine to twelve months of pregnancy.

They dissected the bullfrog and revealed a belly full: Young alligators have been discovered in the innards of bullfrogs. Also, according to Wikipedia:"Wingsuit flying is the art of flying the human body through the air using a special jumpsuit, called a wingsuit, that shapes the human body into an airfoil, which can create lift. The wingsuit creates the airfoil shape with fabric sewn between the legs and under the arms. It is usually incorrectly referenced by the public as a birdman suit or squirrel suit." My friend Thomas says that these high-flyers look like wizards in the sky. Early wingsuits were made of canvas, wood, silk, steel and even whale bone and, not surprising, weren't very reliable. Between 1930 and 1961, 72 of the 75 original wizards died testing their wingsuits—this isn't a verified fact, I just read it on Wikipedia, but it seems plausible.

Fire, earth, water, bicycle: The curse of Undine is a medical condition in which the central nervous system fails to control breathing while a person is asleep. Someone with Undine's curse has no problems breathing while they are awake but their involuntary control is impaired when they hit the pillow. Undine was a water sprite smitten by a knight. She was condemned to stay awake in order to keep breathing. Dolphins are able to send one half of their brain to sleep at a time so that they are never completely unconscious. The other half of the brain monitors what's going on, ensuring that the animal stays out of danger and continues to breathe. These mammals, unlike us, actually do sleep with one eye open.

Note: The sources used for this book only exist temporarily. Please go to Wikipedia to correct inaccuracies.

Acknowledgments: Always, my family—Rachel Dierolf, Fred Dierolf, Marc Hiemstra, Stella terHart Hiemstra, Joshua Hiemstra, Johanna Kuyvenhoven, Andrew Kuyvenhoven and Ena Kuyvenhoven. And always, Caroline Andrews, Nan Gregory, Laura Hunse and Lisa Matin-deMoor—you teach me how to live in this world and how to negotiate with the others.

Poems originally published elsewhere:
"there's an albino pigeon that lands from time to time" has been published in *Arc*. It was also a runner-up for the *Malahat*'s Open Season Poetry Award in 2011. "The most beautiful things I've seen in October" is published in Tightrope's *Best Canadian Poetry in English* (2011) and in *sub-Terrain* (2010). It was also the winner of the Vancouver International Writers and Readers Festival poetry competition (2009). "The day Mom failed to rescue Icarus from the Dutch" appears in *Prairie Fire,* (30.2, 2009), "I'm afraid and it's not just the disappearance of bees" appears in *Grain* (36.3, 2009), and "I told my first stranger I was pregnant" was originally published by *Room* (33.1, 2010) and also won the *Room Magazine* Annual Poetry Competition in 2009. "Browsing *Frog and Toad* together" appears in *Approaches to Poetry: the Pre-Poem Moment,* published by Frog Hollow Press (2009, edited by Shane Neilson). It was also a runner-up for the Mslexia Women's Poetry Competition (U.K.) in the same year.

Jessica Hiemstra is a visual artist and writer. She is also the winner of two *Malahat Review* Open Season Awards (2011) and the *Room Magazine* Annual Poetry Contest (2009). *Self-Portrait Without a Bicycle* is her second full-length volume of poetry.

photograph by Caroline Andrews